D1432610

WEATHER

Wind

by Ann Herriges

BELLWETHER MEDIA • MINNEAPOLIS, MN

Note to Librarians, Teachers, and Parents:

Blastoff! Readers are carefully developed by literacy experts and combine standards-based content with developmentally appropriate text.

Level 1 provides the most support through repetition of high-frequency words, light text, predictable sentence patterns, and strong visual support.

Level 2 offers early readers a bit more challenge through varied simple sentences, increased text load, and less repetition of high-frequency words.

Level 3 advances early-fluent readers toward fluency through increased text and concept load, less reliance on visuals, longer sentences, and more literary language.

Whichever book is right for your reader, Blastoff! Readers are the perfect books to build confidence and encourage a love of reading that will last a lifetime!

This edition first published in 2007 by Bellwether Media.

No part of this publication may be reproduced in whole or in part without written permission of the publisher. For information regarding permission, write to Bellwether Media Inc., Attention: Permissions Department, Post Office Box 1C, Minnetonka, MN 55345-9998.

Library of Congress Cataloging-in-Publication Data
Herriges, Ann.
  Wind / by Ann Herriges.
    p. cm. – (Blastoff! readers) (Weather)
Summary: "Simple text and supportive images introduce beginning readers to the characteristics of wind. Intended for students in kindergarten through third grade."
  Includes bibliographical references and index.
  ISBN-10: 1-60014-026-2 (hardcover : alk. paper)
  ISBN-13: 978-1-60014-026-6 (hardcover : alk. paper
  1. Winds–Juvenile literature. 2. Weather–Juvenile literature. I. Title. II. Series.

  QC931.4.H476 2007
  551.51'8–dc22   2006000617

Text copyright © 2007 by Bellwether Media.
Printed in the United States of America.

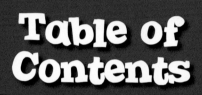

Table of Contents

Wind is moving **air**. It swirls around the earth.

Wind cannot be seen. But you can feel it touch your skin and pull at your clothes.

The sun helps make wind.
Sunshine heats some parts of
the land and sea more than others.

The air grows warmer above these heated areas. Warm air is light. It rises into the sky.

Cold air is heavy. It flows into spots where the warm air was. This movement of air makes the wind blow.

Sometimes the wind hardly moves. The air feels still. Smoke from a chimney rises straight into the air.

Sometimes the wind moves slowly. A **breeze** stirs the leaves on the trees and the hair on your head.

Sometimes the wind moves faster. It pushes sailboats across the water. It tosses kites in the sky.

The wind grows strong when a storm is coming. Dark **clouds** move across the sky.

The wind whips tree branches back and forth. It can turn your umbrella inside out.

Some storms can make **tornadoes**. These powerful winds twist from a cloud down to the ground.

Tornadoes can pull large trees out of the ground. They can lift cars and rip apart buildings.

Blizzards are snowstorms with strong, cold winds. It is hard to walk into the wind in a blizzard.

The wind can blow snow into giant **drifts**.

Hurricanes are huge storms that form over the ocean. They have powerful winds.

eye

Hurricanes are shaped like doughnuts. Winds spin around a hole in the middle called an **eye**.

Hurricanes hit land with great force. The wind pushes tall waves on shore. It can blow down trees and buildings.

A strong wind can turn back into a gentle breeze. The wind is always changing. It carries weather around the earth.

Glossary

air—a mixture of gases around the earth that cannot be seen

blizzard—a snowstorm with strong winds, heavy snow, and cold temperatures

breeze—a gentle wind

cloud—tiny drops of water or crystals of ice that float together in the air

drift—a pile of snow made by the wind

eye—the calm, clear center of a hurricane

hurricane—a powerful, spinning storm with very strong winds; hurricanes form over the Atlantic Ocean and the Caribbean Sea.

sunshine—light from the sun

tornado—a fast-moving, whirling wind that touches the ground; a tornado looks like a dark, cone-shaped cloud.

To Learn More

AT THE LIBRARY
Bauer, Marion Dane. *Wind*. New York: Aladdin, 2003.

Cobb, Vicki. *I Face the Wind*. New York: HarperCollins, 2003.

Gibbons, Gail. *Weather Words and What They Mean*. New York: Holiday House, 1990.

Karas, G. Brian. *The Windy Day*. New York: Simon & Schuster, 1998.

ON THE WEB
Learning more about the weather is as easy as 1, 2, 3.

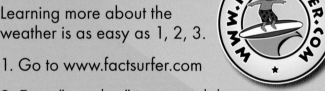

1. Go to www.factsurfer.com

2. Enter "weather" into search box.

3. Click the "Surf" button and you will see a list of related web sites.

With factsurfer.com, finding more information is just a click away.

Index

The photographs in this book are reproduced through the courtesy of: Laurie Stracan/Alamy, front cover; NPA/Getty Images, p. 4; Gloria-Leigh Logan, p. 5; Angelo Cavalli/Getty Images, pp. 6, 18-19; Michael Busselle/Getty Images, p. 7; Jim Cummins/Getty Images, p. 8; Jean-Marc Truchet, p. 9; Simone van den Berg, p. 10; stevegeer, p. 11; maodesign, p. 11(inset); Chris Windsor/Getty Images, pp. 12-13; Carsten Peter/Getty Images, pp. 14-15; altrendo nature/Getty Images, p. 16; Comstock Royalty Free, p. 17; Juan Martinez, p. 19; Ken Briggs/Getty Images, p. 20; Martin Barraud, p. 21.